Classic Collection

Heidi

Johanna Spyri

Adapted by Ronne Randall • Illustrated by Iva Sasheva

QEB Publishing

Up to the Mountain

One bright, sunny summer morning, a five-year-old girl climbed the winding path leading up to the Alm mountain in Switzerland. Her name was Heidi, and her parents had died when she was a baby. Since then, she had been looked after by her Aunt Dete, who now walked beside her.

On the way up, Dete's friend Barbel came out to say hello. "Where are you taking Heidi?" she asked.

"Up to her grandfather's," Dete replied.

"The old man everyone calls the Alm-Uncle?" Barbel exclaimed. "He'll never be able to look after her!"

"I have no choice," Dete said sadly. "I have a new job in Frankfurt, and I can't take Heidi with me."

"But the Alm-Uncle is almost a hermit—we never see him in the village or at church," said Barbel. "All he has are his two goats. How will he provide for her?"

"He's Heidi's grandfather. She will be fine with him," Dete insisted. She looked around. "Now, where is she?"

"There, I see her!" cried Barbel. "She is with Peter, the boy who looks after the goats."

A short distance away, Heidi was walking with a boy a few years older than she was. The two children were barefoot, chatting happily and laughing together while a herd of goats scampered nearby. Dete smiled as she watched them. "I think Heidi will feel right at home here," she told Barbel, sounding very relieved.

Heidi's grandfather was a gruff old man. He was not pleased when Dete left the young girl with him.

But Heidi was enchanted with her new surroundings. She gazed at the pine trees and listened to the wind singing as it moved through the branches.

Grandfather picked up the bundle of Heidi's clothes that Aunt Dete had left. "We'd better put these away inside," he said. "Don't you want to put your shoes on?"

"No, I want to walk around like the goats!" said Heidi.

For the first time in years, Grandfather smiled. "So you will," he said.

Grandfather's house was just one room, with his bed in the corner. Heidi wondered where she would sleep.

"Sleep wherever you wish," said Grandfather.

There was a ladder that led up to the hayloft, and Heidi climbed it. When she discovered all of the soft, sweet-smelling hay, she cried out with delight.

"I'll sleep up here!" she said.

Grandfather brought up a sheet to put over the hay, as well as a blanket to keep Heidi warm.

At suppertime, Grandfather made a simple meal of bread and cheese. He ladled some fresh, creamy goat's milk into a mug for Heidi, and she drank it eagerly.

"I have never tasted such delicious milk!" she declared.

That night, as she snuggled into her bed, Heidi could see the moon shining down through the little window of the hayloft. She fell asleep to the sound of the wind whistling through the pines, a sweet smile on her face.

In the Pasture

A shrill whistle woke Heidi up the next morning. She opened her eyes to the bright sunlight streaming in through her little window. Excited, she jumped out of bed, dressed quickly, and ran outside.

Peter, the goat herder she had met the day before, was waiting for Grandfather to bring his goats out to join the herd.

"Would you like to go to the pasture with Peter and the goats?" Grandfather asked Heidi.

"Oh, yes, please!" said Heidi enthusiastically.

Grandfather packed them some food and milk. Then Peter, Heidi, and the goats set off up the Alm.

All morning, Heidi scampered among the brightly colored wildflowers and played with the goats. Little Swan and Little Bear, who belonged to Grandfather, were Heidi's favorites.

Peter showed her where an eagle had its nest on a rocky cliff, and they watched it soar into the air. Heidi spotted snowfields higher up the mountain, icy white against the deep blue sky. She was amazed by all she saw.

At noon, they sat under a pine tree and ate the lunch Grandfather had packed. Heidi very quickly drank all of her milk, so Peter got her some more, straight from Little Swan. It was warm and sweet and delicious.

Late in the afternoon, when the sunset turned the sky to fire, Heidi and Peter made their way back down from the pasture. Heidi had never been happier.

Peter's Grandmother

Heidi went to the pasture with Peter and the goats every day that summer. She and Peter became good friends, and Heidi grew strong and healthy in the fresh mountain air.

When the fall winds began to blow, Heidi went up the mountain less and less. When the winter arrived and snow covered the Alm, Peter went to school down in the village of Dörfli. He told Heidi that his grandmother found the winter days lonely and that Heidi should visit.

Heidi pestered her reluctant grandfather until eventually he bundled her into blankets, set her on his old wooden sled, and took her to Peter's cottage. Anxious to avoid Peter's family, he left Heidi at the door.

Peter's mother welcomed Heidi and showed her to Peter's grandmother, who sat at a spinning wheel. On hearing that the old woman was blind, Heidi was upset at the thought that she could no longer see the beautiful snowy mountains. So she held her hand and described the scene from the cottage window as best as she could.

"Tell me about your grandfather, Heidi," said Peter's grandmother. "I knew him when we were younger."

Heidi talked fondly of Grandfather, how he could make anything out of wood, and how much she had enjoyed the summer in Alm. The old woman listened intently, surprised at how happy the little girl seemed.

Heidi came to visit often that winter, brightening the old woman's days.

Visitors

The years passed quickly and happily for Heidi, and by the time she was eight years old, she had learned many things from her grandfather.

One spring morning, the pastor from Dörfli came to see Grandfather.

"Heidi needs an education," the pastor said. "Move down to the village next winter so that she can go to school with the other children. It will be good for you to live among your neighbors again." Grandfather refused.

"Heidi does not need to go to school," he said. "She is happy here and doesn't need other children." Shaking his head at the old man's stubbornness, the pastor left.

The next day, Aunt Dete came to see them.

"I am taking Heidi back to Frankfurt with me," she told Grandfather. Dete then explained that she knew of a young girl who could not walk and spent her days in a wheelchair. Her father was looking for a bright little girl to be her companion, and Heidi would be perfect.

Heidi was distraught and refused to leave. Grandfather did not want her to leave either, but Dete insisted that she would enjoy Frankfurt.

"Take her, then," snapped Grandfather angrily, "and don't ever come back!"

Dete and Heidi left in a rush. Heidi wanted to say good-bye to everyone, but Dete said there was no time.

"You can bring them presents from Frankfurt," she said. Convinced she would soon return, Heidi followed Dete.

A New Life for Heidi

Clara Sesemann sat in her wheelchair in the library of her house in Frankfurt, as she did every day. Her mother had died years ago, and her father was often away on business, so Clara was looked after by a strict woman named Miss Rottenmeier. Miss Rottenmeier sat sewing calmly, while Clara fidgeted and fretted. She had been waiting all day for Heidi to arrive.

"When will they get here?" she asked for the tenth time in an hour. At that moment, the door opened, and a servant brought in Heidi and Aunt Dete.

"Hmmm," sniffed Miss Rottenmeier, studying Heidi through disapproving eyes. "She looks far too young. Clara is twelve years old, and we expected a companion of her own age. How old is Heidi?"

"Er…" Dete hesitated. "I'm not sure exactly…"

"I am eight years old," Heidi declared.

"And what books have you read?" Miss Rottenmeier asked, sounding somewhat scary.

"I haven't read any," Heidi replied. "I can't read yet."

Miss Rottenmeier was shocked and remained silent.

"You can have lessons with me, Heidi," Clara said gently. "The Professor is kind, but his lessons can be a bit boring. If we have them together, it will be fun."

She smiled warmly. Heidi liked Clara, but Miss Rottenmeier had been very unwelcoming, and Heidi really wasn't sure she would like her new life.

The End of a Long Day

Aunt Dete left quickly, and Heidi stayed with Clara until it was time for dinner. A servant named Sebastian came to push Clara's wheelchair into the large and ornate dining room.

Heidi had never seen such fine plates or such a beautiful tablecloth. She was pleased to see a soft white roll next to her plate. Peter's grandmother loved this type of bread.

"I can take her one as a present," Heidi thought, slipping the roll into her pocket.

When Sebastian served Heidi some meat, she looked up at him and asked, "Is all that for me?"

Trying not to smile, Sebastian nodded.

"Heidi, mind your manners!" scolded Miss Rottenmeier. "I see you have a lot to learn! You must never speak to the servants."

Miss Rottenmeier continued telling Heidi the rules she was to follow: how to enter and leave a room, how to keep her things tidy, how to eat properly… Miss Rottenmeier droned on for so long that Heidi fell asleep in her chair. She was very, very tired!

"Never in my life have I come across anything like this child!" Miss Rottenmeier shouted. Clara began to giggle, which made Miss Rottenmeier even angrier.

But not even the shouting and laughter woke Heidi up, and she had to be carried to her room and put to bed. Her first day in Frankfurt was over.

When Heidi woke up the next morning, she did not remember where she was. Looking through the window, she could see no grass and no pine trees—only tall buildings. This gave her a strange, sad feeling.

After breakfast, Clara's kind and patient teacher, the Professor, arrived. Miss Rottenmeier was eager to tell him how much Heidi had to learn.

"She cannot even read!" she said. "I am sure she will hold Clara back in her studies."

But the Professor calmly assured her that he could teach both girls. He would start by teaching Heidi the alphabet. Defeated, Miss Rottenmeier left in a huff.

Moments later, there was a crash in the schoolroom, and Miss Rottenmeier rushed back in. A table lay on its side, schoolbooks were scattered, and a stream of black ink ran across the carpet. Heidi was nowhere to be seen.

"What has that troublesome child done now?" the furious Miss Rottenmeier demanded.

"It was an accident," Clara explained. "Heidi heard something in the street and ran so quickly to see what it was that she bumped into the table. It wasn't her fault."

Miss Rottenmeier found Heidi standing at the front door, looking outside in confusion.

"I thought I heard the wind rushing through the pines," she explained. "But I can't see any trees."

"Do you think we live in a forest, foolish girl?" Miss Rottenmeier snapped. "If this ever happens again, you will be punished. Do you understand?"

"Yes," said Heidi. "I promise to sit still from now on."

The Church Tower

In the afternoon, when Clara was resting, Heidi sneaked out of the house, hoping to find a place where she could see the mountains she loved.

She met a friendly boy about her own age playing a barrel organ, and she asked him if he knew of such a place.

"You can try going to the top of the church tower," he suggested. "I'll show you if you like."

When they got to the church, Heidi knocked on the door. It was opened by a caretaker, who didn't believe that Heidi wanted to climb the tower. He was about to send her away, but her eyes were so full of longing that he changed his mind.

"Come with me," he said, leading her up a narrow, winding staircase. When they reached the top, the caretaker held Heidi up to the tiny window so that she could look out.

Heidi couldn't see any mountains anywhere.

"It's not what I expected," she said sadly.

When they got downstairs, Heidi spotted a basket near the caretaker's room. In it was a large calico cat with seven kittens nestled beside her.

"How sweet they are!" Heidi exclaimed. Her face lit up with such delight that the caretaker said she could keep two of them.

"One for me and one for Clara," she said, tucking them into her pockets.

Heidi found her way back home and rang the doorbell. Sebastian came at once and whispered, "Come in quickly! They have all gone in to dinner, and Miss Rottenmeier is furious!"

Heidi tried to slip into the dining room unnoticed, but Miss Rottenmeier said sternly, "Your behavior has been shocking, Heidi. You will be punished for leaving the house without permission and staying out so late. What do you have to say for yourself?"

"Meow!" came the surprising reply.

"Heidi!" shouted Miss Rottenmeier. "Do you dare to be saucy on top of all of your other misbehavior?"

"I'm not being saucy," Heidi protested meekly.

"Meow! Meow!"

"This is too much!" cried Miss Rottenmeier, standing up. "Leave the room at once!" she said sternly.

"Please," Heidi begged, "it's not me. It's the kittens."

"Kittens?" screeched Miss Rottenmeier. "*Kittens*? Sebastian! Come here at once and get rid of the horrible creatures!" She stormed out of the room.

By this time, both of the fluffy kittens were on Clara's lap, and she and Heidi were playing with them.

"Sebastian, please help us," Clara said. "We want to keep the kittens and play with them whenever we can. Can you find a place to hide them?"

"Don't worry, Miss Clara," Sebastian replied. "I'll keep them in a basket in the attic. They'll be safe there."

The girls smiled happily at each other.

Grandmama

Although Heidi was now good friends with Clara, she was still very homesick. She talked to Clara about Peter and the goats every day, and every day she said, "I must go home soon." She kept saving rolls for Peter's grandmother and was heartbroken when Miss Rottenmeier found them and threw them away.

One day, Clara told Heidi that her Grandmama was coming to stay for a while. "Everyone loves her, and I'm sure you will, too, Heidi," Clara said.

Clara was right. Grandmama had a kind smile and merry, twinkling eyes. Heidi liked her at once. Every afternoon, while Clara was resting, Grandmama sat with Heidi and read to her.

One day, Grandmama opened a book that had beautiful pictures of green fields where sheep and goats grazed. Looking at it, Heidi burst into loud sobs.

"You are missing the mountains, aren't you?" said Grandmama, putting her arm around Heidi.

Heidi nodded miserably.

"When you can read this wonderful book for yourself, it will be yours," Grandmama promised.

Just a few days later, the Professor told Grandmama that something astonishing had happened: Heidi could read! That evening at dinnertime, Heidi found the beautiful book next to her plate.

"It is yours to keep forever," said Grandmama with a twinkle in her eyes.

The House Is Haunted

When Grandmama's visit ended, Heidi's homesickness got worse. She lost her appetite and grew very pale. Every night she cried herself to sleep.

One morning, the servants came downstairs to find the front door wide open. Thinking a thief had gotten in, they searched every corner of the house. Nothing was missing. When it happened again the next day, Sebastian said he would sit up that night to keep watch.

Just after midnight, Sebastian heard a loud *whoosh* as the front door was opened. He ran out and saw a ghostly figure in white disappearing up the stairs.

The next morning, all of the servants were talking about the ghost. When Mr. Sesemann heard the story, he invited Dr. Classen, the family doctor, to sit with him and wait for this "ghost" to appear.

That night, when the figure in white came downstairs to open the door, Mr. Sesemann and Dr. Classen were waiting for her. It was Heidi, walking in her sleep, looking just like a ghost.

"Dear child, what are you doing?" asked Mr. Sesemann softly, so as not to startle the girl.

Heidi's eyes flew open, and she looked confused. "I don't know," she said, beginning to cry.

The pale young girl told Dr. Classen about her sadness and how much she missed Grandfather and the Alm.

"There is only one thing to do," Dr. Classen told Mr. Sesemann later. "I'm afraid Heidi must go home."

Home to the Alm

The next morning, Miss Rottenmeier was told to pack Heidi's things. Clara was very upset at losing her new friend, but her father promised her that they could visit Heidi the following summer.

After breakfast, Clara gave Heidi a basket of fresh, soft white rolls for Peter's grandmother. And Mr. Sesemann gave her an envelope for her grandfather.

"Be sure to keep it safe," he said kindly.

Sebastian took the train with Heidi all the way to Dörfli. There her trunk was put on a cart to be delivered to Grandfather's hut. Heidi assured Sebastian she could walk up the mountain alone, which she did.

On her way up, Heidi stopped at Peter's cottage. Grandmother was overjoyed that Heidi was back. Heidi gave her the white rolls, saying, "Now you won't have to eat hard bread for a few days!"

Grandmother hugged her and said, "What blessings you bring! But the greatest blessing of all is you yourself."

After a while, Heidi continued her walk up the Alm. Before long, she could see the hut, and there, sitting on his bench and smoking his pipe, was Grandfather.

Heidi raced up and threw her arms around his neck, saying over and over, "Grandfather! Grandfather!" The old man's eyes filled with tears, and he hugged her as if he would never let her go.

"I've come home, Grandfather," said Heidi, "and I'm never going away again."

Heidi gave Grandfather the envelope from Mr. Sesemann. Inside there was a letter explaining why Heidi had come home, along with some money for her.

Grandfather wanted to use the money to buy Heidi a proper bed, but she said she would rather buy a soft white roll for Grandmother every morning.

Eager to show Grandfather how well she could read, Heidi took down a big Bible and read to him from it. Grandfather was pleased and proud, and as the next day was Sunday, he promised to take her to church in Dörfli.

So the next morning, as the church bells rang out from the village, Heidi and Grandfather walked down to Dörfli hand in hand. Everyone was surprised and happy to see Grandfather, as he had not been to church for many years.

After the mass, Grandfather stopped to talk to the pastor. "I have thought about your advice," he said, "and I realize now that you were right. I hope you will forgive me for being so stubborn. We will be moving down to Dörfli this winter so that Heidi can go to school."

As they left the church, many of the villagers crowded around to welcome Grandfather back to Dörfli. Heidi had never seen him smile so much. On their way home, Heidi and Grandfather stopped to tell Peter, his mother, and his grandmother the good news.

"I am glad you are back," said Peter.

"We will be going to school together," Heidi told Peter happily. "I can't wait!"

News for Clara

In Frankfurt, Clara was so looking forward to visiting Heidi. But as the summer drew near, Dr. Classen had some bad news for her.

"I'm afraid you're not strong enough to make the journey, my dear," the kind doctor told Clara and her father gently.

Choking back her sobs, Clara said, "Please, Dr. Classen, will you go instead?"

"But Clara, what will I do there?" the doctor asked in a surprised voice.

"Everything I would do!" exclaimed Clara. "You can meet Heidi's grandfather and Peter and the goats and then tell me all about it. And you can bring everyone the presents I have been saving for them. Please, Dr. Classen," she begged, grabbing the doctor's hand. "If you do, I promise to take all of the cod liver oil you want me to, every day!"

The doctor laughed. "Well, if you promise that, I can hardly refuse, can I? When should I go?"

"Tomorrow!" exclaimed Clara, smiling now.

Clara very carefully packed the presents: a warm woolen cape for Heidi; a cozy shawl and a box of cakes for Peter's grandmother; some pipe tobacco for Heidi's grandfather; and delicious sausages for everyone. She couldn't wait to hear how Heidi liked her present. She would make sure the doctor told her everything!

Grandfather was in the shed, milking the goats, when Heidi rushed in, her face glowing with excitement.

"They're coming! Dr. Classen is coming! Clara and Grandmama must be right behind him!" She turned and ran back to greet the guests from Frankfurt.

But when Dr. Classen arrived, he was all alone. Heidi was filled with disappointment when he explained why Clara and Grandmama were not with him.

"Perhaps Clara will be well enough to come next spring," he told Heidi, not really believing it himself.

Grandfather welcomed the doctor with a hearty handshake and a delicious lunch of goat's milk, cheese, and cold meat.

"This is better than anything I have ever tasted in Frankfurt," Dr. Classen remarked.

Grandfather smiled proudly. "This is what Clara needs," he said. "Wholesome food and fresh mountain air would do wonders for the girl, I'm sure of it."

After lunch, a man delivered a large box—it was filled with the gifts from Clara. Heidi opened each present with a look of delight. The most exciting present of all was the box of cakes for Peter's grandmother.

"I want to take them to her right now!" said Heidi.

As they all walked down the path to Peter's cottage, Heidi declared, "Nothing has made me happier than the doctor's visit."

Dr. Classen laughed, but inside he was deeply moved by Heidi's words.

School Days

In October, barely a month after Dr. Classen's visit, snow began falling on the mountain, and Grandfather, Heidi, and the goats moved down to Dörfli. Grandfather had found an old, tumbledown house near the church and had divided it into two sections, one for the goats and one for himself and Heidi. There was a big stove to keep the whole house warm and cozy, and there were lovely pictures on the walls for Heidi to look at.

Heidi started going to school, which she enjoyed very much. She knew that Peter came down to school on his sled, and she was looking forward to seeing him there. But Peter often stayed away from school, even on sunny days when it would have been easy for him to get there.

"Why don't you come to school more often?" Heidi asked him one day. Peter was embarrassed and didn't want to answer at first.

"I have never learned how to read," he finally confessed. "And so I find school difficult."

"You can learn," Heidi told him. "I can teach you."

Peter grumbled, but Heidi convinced him that he would be able to do it. She started by teaching him the alphabet, just as the Professor had done in Frankfurt.

Peter started coming to school more regularly, and every afternoon he sat with Heidi learning new letters and words. By the middle of the winter, Peter was able to read to his grandmother from her hymnbook, which made her very happy.

A Letter

The winter in Dörfli passed happily for Heidi. Before she knew it, May had arrived, and the mountain streams, fed by all of the melted snow, rushed and leaped down into the valley. It was time for Heidi and Grandfather to go back to their home high up on the Alm.

Heidi ran everywhere, looking for new wildflowers in the grass, feeling the warm sun on her cheeks, and listening to the wind rushing through the pines. She hadn't realized how much she had missed everything.

Peter was back, too, looking after the goats. They were also pleased to be on the mountain, grazing on the new green grass. Heidi rushed out to meet Peter every morning, happy that they would be spending carefree days together again.

One morning, Peter had something for Heidi. "The mailman gave me this to give to you," he said. It was from Clara! Excited, Heidi ran to read it to Grandfather.

"Dear Heidi," the letter began, "we are coming to see you! We hope to come in six weeks, after I have had some treatments. Father needs to be in Paris, but Grandmama will be with me. I can hardly wait!"

Heidi was relieved to read that Miss Rottenmeier would be staying in Frankfurt. The letter was signed, "Your true friend, Clara."

Heidi thought she would burst with happiness. Clara would be coming to her mountain at last!

Then one day in June, Heidi saw a strange procession winding its way up the Alm. Two men were carrying a wheelchair on poles, and in the chair sat Clara, well wrapped in blankets and shawls. Behind her was Grandmama, on horseback.

"They're here!" cried Heidi, rushing to get Grandfather. Together, they made their way down to greet their guests.

As Clara's chair was gently set down, she gazed around in wonder. "It's so beautiful!" she said. "I wish I could run around and see everything with you, Heidi!"

"I'll show it all to you," said Heidi. She pushed Clara's chair to the pines so that Clara could hear the wind rushing through them. Then she took Clara to see her favorite goats, Little Swan and Little Bear, in their stalls.

At lunchtime, Grandmama couldn't believe how the fresh mountain air had given Clara such a good appetite.

Later that day, Heidi showed Clara and Grandmama her bed in the sweet-smelling hayloft.

"What a wonderful bedroom you have!" exclaimed Clara. "The hay looks so soft, and the blue sky is right outside your window."

"If Grandmama agrees," said Grandfather, "we would be very happy for you to stay for a few weeks."

Grandmama smiled. "I think it would do her good," she said. "And I thank you with all of my heart."

Heidi and Clara beamed at each other, and started planning all of the things they would do together.

The next morning, Heidi and Clara sat outside the hut. Clara breathed in the scent of the pine trees—she already felt better than she had in Frankfurt.

Grandfather brought out mugs of fresh, creamy milk for the girls. "This is from Little Swan," he said. "Drink up, Clara. It will give you strength!"

Soon Peter arrived, expecting Heidi to join him.

"Clara is here, so I can't come today," she explained, "or tomorrow or the day after. Grandfather has said that he might take both of us up to the pasture one day, but for now I am staying here with Clara."

Peter scowled but said nothing. He turned and drove the goats up the mountain as fast as he could, never once looking back.

Heidi and Clara had promised to write to Grandmama every day, so Heidi brought out everything they needed from the house, and they wrote their letters in the warm sunshine.

Grandfather said that Clara needed lots of sunshine and fresh air. After lunch, Heidi took Clara's chair to a shady spot under a tree, where the warm breeze ruffled their hair. They spent the afternoon telling each other everything that had happened since they had last been together.

As the sun began to set, Heidi saw Peter bringing the goats down and called to him. But he did not answer or even turn his head.

A Present from Grandmama

Over the next few weeks, Grandfather took Clara out in her chair every morning, and she and Heidi spent the day outside. And every morning Grandfather said to Clara kindly, "Will you try to stand today?"

To please him, Clara always tried, holding his arm for support. "Oh, it hurts!" she would cry. But every day, Grandfather gently encouraged her to stand for a few seconds longer.

The girls had breakfast and lunch outside. Clara loved the goat's milk Grandfather gave them, and she drank hers even more quickly than Heidi did.

With all of the fresh air and good food, Clara slept very well at night and always woke up happy and well rested. One day, the girls saw two men coming up the mountain, each carrying a bed on his back. They also had fresh white sheets and blankets and pillows— and a letter from Grandmama.

The letter said that the beds were for Heidi and Clara. Heidi was to take hers to the house in Dörfli so that she would be warm in the winter, and Clara's could stay in Grandfather's hut ready for her next visit.

Grandfather cleared the hay from the hayloft and helped the men take the beds up the ladder to the loft. He placed them perfectly so that both girls could see equally well out of the window.

"From now on, we will both sleep in proper beds!" said Heidi joyfully, and the two girls laughed.

First Steps

One bright morning, Grandfather agreed to take both girls up to the pasture where Peter grazed the goats. He brought Clara's wheelchair outside and then went back into the hut to get the girls.

At that moment, Peter came by. Ever since Clara had arrived and taken Heidi away from him, Peter had felt angry. When he saw Clara's wheelchair, his anger burst out, and he pushed the chair as hard as he could, smiling grimly as he watched it tumble down the mountainside and shatter into pieces.

Grandfather wondered what had happened to the chair, but he assured the girls that they could still go up to the pasture. He carried Clara there, gently placing her on a blanket on the sunny grass next to Heidi. When Peter saw them, he scowled and turned away.

"I wish you could see the wildflowers, Clara," Heidi said a while later. "Maybe Peter and I can carry you over to look at them."

Peter still wanted nothing to do with Clara, but when he saw that she really could not stand, he felt sorry for what he had done and agreed to help her. Together, Heidi and Peter managed to get Clara to stand. Then Heidi gently coaxed her to take a step.

"It hurts," Clara said, "but not as much as it used to!" Bravely, Clara took another step and another. "Heidi, look!" she cried. "I can do it! I can walk!"

Grandmama was coming to get Clara in a week's time, and every day for the next week, Grandfather and Heidi helped Clara take a few more steps.

When Grandmama finally arrived, she could hardly recognize Clara. "Your cheeks are so round and rosy!" she exclaimed. "And where is your chair?"

In reply, Heidi helped Clara stand. Together, they walked to Grandmama, their faces beaming.

Grandmama gasped. Then, laughing and crying at the same time, she embraced Clara with joy.

The next day, there was a big surprise for Clara— her father arrived from Paris! When he saw his daughter walking toward him, he was too overcome to speak. He folded Clara in his arms and kissed her again and again.

"We can never thank you and Heidi enough," Mr. Sesemann told Grandfather later. "Tell me your dearest wish, and it will be yours."

Grandfather said his reward was seeing Clara grow so healthy, but Heidi asked that Peter's grandmother have her bed from Frankfurt. She wanted her to be warm during the winter. Mr. Sesemann was happy to help.

Sadly, it was time to say good-bye. The girls hugged, and Clara promised she would be back next summer.

Heidi waved to her friends until they were out of sight. Then she took Grandfather's hand, and together they walked home, both happy and content. Heidi's kindness had brought joy to so many people, but she had transformed her grandfather's life most of all.

About the author

Johanna Louise Spyri was born in 1827 in Hirzel,
a small mountain village in Switzerland. She was one of
six children and grew up in a house full of books and music.
She married at the age of 25 and had one son.
In her later years, Johanna loved to travel, and she spent most
of her adult life working for charities. *Heidi* was based on the
Alpine countryside where Johanna spent many childhood
summers. Published when she was 54, its huge success
took her by surprise. Johanna died in 1901 at the age of 74.
Although she had written more than 25 books in her lifetime,
it is the kindhearted Heidi who will forever be loved
around the world.

Other titles in the *Classic Collection* series:

Alice's Adventures in Wonderland • *Little Women*
The Three Musketeers • *Treasure Island*
20,000 Leagues Under the Sea • *Pinocchio* • *The Wizard of Oz*

Editors: Joanna Pocock and Victoria Garrard • Designer: Andrea Mills

Copyright © QEB Publishing 2012

First published in the United States in 2012 by
QEB Publishing, Inc.
3 Wrigley, Suite A
Irvine, CA 92618

www.qed-publishing.co.uk

A CIP record for this book is available from the Library of Congress.

ISBN 978 1 60992 418 8

Printed in China